Writing Tip: Never use two words where one will do.

Robert Quackenbush

PASS THE QUILL, I'LL WRITE A DRAFT

✦ A Story of Thomas Jefferson ✦

 PIPPIN PRESS
NEW YORK

Published by Pippin Press, Gracie Station Box #92,
229 East 85th Street, New York, N.Y. 10028

Printed in Spain by Novograph, S.A., Madrid.

10 9 8 7 6 5 4 3 2 1

Library of Congress Cataloging-in-Publication Data

Quackenbush, Robert M.
    Pass the quill : I'll write a draft : a story of Thomas
Jefferson / written and illustrated by Robert Quackenbush.
        p.   cm.
    Summary: Follows the life and accomplishments of the third
president, from his birth in 1743 to his retirement to Monticello.
    ISBN 0-945912-07-2.
    1. Jefferson, Thomas, 1743-1826—Juvenile literature.
2. Jefferson, Thomas, 1743-1826—Juvenile humor.   3. Presidents-
-United States—Biography—Juvenile literature.   4. Presidents-
-United States—Biography—Juvenile humor.   [1. Jefferson, Thomas,
1743-1826.   2. Presidents.]   I. Title.
E332.79.Q33   1989
973.4'6'092—dc20
[B]
[92]   89-8439
                                                              CIP
                                                               AC

For Piet, Margie,
& Barbara

There was once a boy named Thomas Jefferson. He was born on April 13, 1743 on his parents' plantation, called Shadwell, in central Virginia. In those days, Virginia was one of thirteen American colonies ruled by Great Britain. Thomas had two older sisters, four younger sisters, and three younger brothers. His mother, Jane Randolph Jefferson, was the daughter of a wealthy planter. His father, Peter Randolph, was a prominent landowner, surveyor, and mapmaker. Peter was a strong, powerful man who enjoyed exploring the Virginia wilderness. When out on these adventures, he would eat raw game and sleep in hollow trees away from wolves. He taught Thomas how to ride a horse, use a gun, and how to survive on his own in the wilderness. But there was one thing that he wanted Thomas to have that he, himself, lacked—a formal education. So young Thomas was taught by tutors until he was nine. Then he went to boarding school fifty miles away. "Never use two words where one will do," said one of his teachers. And Thomas never forgot the rule.

When Thomas was fourteen, his father died. Thomas moved to a boarding school closer to Shadwell, so he could be with his family on weekends. His teacher, Reverend James Maury, taught him to read ancient classics in the original Greek and Latin. During his free time, the tall, red-haired Thomas liked to climb an 857-foot peak on the Jefferson property. He called the place Monticello, which in Italian means "little mountain." He would lie under a favorite oak tree and dream about building a house on Monticello one day. But he still had many more years of education ahead of him before he could do that. He continued at boarding school until he was seventeen. Then he enrolled at William and Mary College in Williamsburg. After two years of studying the arts, philosophy, languages, and the classics, Jefferson felt that he had learned all he could. So he went to study law with George Wythe, a successful lawyer and member of Virginia's governing body, called the House of Burgesses. Five years later Jefferson received his license to practice law. He opened an office in Williamsburg.

In May 1769, at the age of twenty six, Jefferson was elected to the House of Burgesses. He seldom spoke out at meetings, because he was shy. His skill was in writing laws and drafting bills. He began his duties by drafting a bill that would make it easier to free slaves. He was opposed to slavery, although he owned slaves himself, as did many other early Virginia families. He believed that all people should be free and equal. Unfortunately, his bill was ahead of its time and it was not passed. Jefferson was very disappointed. Still, he stayed on in politics and kept up with his busy law practice. At the same time he began to build his Monticello dream house. Workmen had just finished a little brick cottage when a tragedy occurred. Early in 1770, the huge wooden house at Shadwell burned to the ground. No one was hurt, but all of Jefferson's books and papers were destroyed. Only his violin, which he played so well, was saved. He moved his mother and four sisters, who were still living at home, to the little brick cottage. Then he proceeded at once to build a mansion on the Monticello property to replace Shadwell.

When Jefferson was twenty-eight, he married Martha Wayles Skelton, a young widow who lived near Williamsburg. The wedding took place in Martha's home on New Year's Day, 1772. Guests came from all over to drink wine punch and eat black wedding cake made with fruits and spices. The celebration lasted two and a half weeks. Then the couple set off for their new home at Monticello, one hundred miles away. They started out by carriage in a snowstorm. Halfway to their destination, a carriage wheel broke. They had to finish the journey on horseback, arriving at Monticello during the night. In order not to awaken a sleeping household in the unfinished mansion, they spent their first night in the tiny brick cottage. Over the next six months they were busy finishing the mansion. Then, the following September their first child, a daughter, was born and Jefferson promptly named her Martha after her mother. A few months later, his wife's father died and left her 11,000 acres of land. Jefferson was forced to sell his law practice in order to have time to manage all the property that he and Martha now owned.

Meanwhile, the American colonists were rebelling against harsh British rule and unfair taxes. On the night of December 16, 1773, some colonists dressed as Native Americans protested a tax on tea. They dumped the tea from three British cargo ships into Boston Harbor. As punishment, the British government closed the harbor and refused to let the Massachusetts legislature hold meetings. In addition, the House of Burgesses was shut down. In all the turmoil, Jefferson became a spokesman for the colonists. He wrote a paper titled, "A Summary View of the Rights of British America." His words expressed brilliantly the complaints of the American colonists against the British Parliament and King. The Virginia lawmakers were very impressed by the paper. They asked Jefferson to be a member of the delegation from Virginia to the First Continental Congress in Philadelphia. This Congress included John Adams, Benjamin Franklin, George Washington, James Madison, Patrick Henry, and other distinguished colonial leaders. Their goal at the first congress was to unite the colonies and air grievances against Great Britain.

THE DECLARATION
COMMITTEE:
Thomas Jefferson, Roger Sherman, Benjamin Franklin, Robert Livingston, & John Adams.

By the spring of 1776, the Revolutionary War was under way and there was no turning back. The Second Continental Congress met and selected George Washington to lead the American forces. From June 11 to June 28, Jefferson composed the Declaration of Independence. His immortal words declared the thirteen colonies—now called the United States of America—to be a free and independent nation. His first draft was his finished document. He delivered it to Congress and a heated debate began. Every word was mulled over. Many words and phases were deleted. Jefferson was horrified that his Declaration was being picked at by men with less writing ability than he had. But he managed to remain silent. Even so, he kept looking at a barometer to see what the temperature was like outside. It was as if he were checking on his own boiling point. In the end his Declaration was unchanged but considerably shortened, so it was still his own work. When it was signed on July 4, 1776, the break with Great Britain was complete. Jefferson wrote down in his notebook that it was 73½ degrees outside.

19

While the Revolutionary War raged in the North, Jefferson remained at home working to make Virginia more democratic. He proudly drafted the Virginia Statute for Religious Freedom, which was passed by the legislature. Then, in June, 1779, the Virginia legislature elected him wartime governor. When the British shifted their military effort to the South toward Richmond, Jefferson moved the Virginia government from Richmond to Charlottesville, near Monticello. But the British kept coming. With the British at his coattails, he had to flee to safety with his family to neighboring plantations, or risk being hanged as a traitor. With only two weeks left in his term as governor, he retired from the office. The British destroyed one of his farms and took over Monticello briefly. When it was safe to return, Jefferson was relieved to see that Monticello had not been damaged. The love he felt for his home and Virginia welled inside him. He began to work on a book called *Notes on the State of Virginia*. He wrote down everything he knew about Virginia from its history to its plants and animals. The book has been considered by many scholars the most important scientific and political book written by an American before 1785.

Jefferson's flight from the British when his term as war governor ended caused an uproar. The Virginia legislature voted to investigate his conduct as governor during the crisis. When it was proved that his conduct was unquestionable, his name was cleared. Even so, Jefferson resigned his seat in the legislature. He also declined to serve in the Continental Congress. His mind was on Monticello and the problems he was having there. Martha became quite ill following the difficult birth of their sixth child, Lucy Elizabeth, in June, 1782. (Three other infants had died at birth, and Lucy was to die of whooping cough eighteen months later). All that summer Jefferson stayed at his wife's side. She became weaker and weaker. On September 6, 1782, she died. Jefferson grieved so much that he would not leave his room for weeks. He would see no one except his children. At last, his grief and despair lessened. He felt that work would relieve his mind of Martha's death, so when he was elected to serve in the new Congress that was meeting that season, he accepted.

The following year, 1783, the Revolutionary War ended. A peace treaty was signed on September 3, 1783. America was now a free and independent nation. Then, in 1784, Congress asked Jefferson to go to Paris to help Benjamin Franklin and John Adams make treaties with the nations of Europe. He gladly accepted. He arranged to have his two surviving children, Martha and Mary, with him. In Paris he met important government leaders and became a favorite of French society. In 1785, Franklin sailed back to America and Adams became America's first ambassador to England. At the same time, Congress chose Jefferson to be America's Ambassador to France. After five years in diplomatic service, Jefferson and his daughters returned to America. His plan was to take care of debts and other affairs at Monticello and then return to France. But as soon as his ship arrived in America, he changed his plans. His country needed his experience for an important new office. George Washington, who was serving his first term as president, wanted his help to run the country. Jefferson became the first secretary of state.

Jefferson found that it was not easy starting the new government. There was a lot of squabbling among the President's cabinet members. Each man had his own ideas about how the new nation established under the Constitution and Bill of Rights should be run. About the only thing Jefferson felt good about was getting everyone to agree on a new capital. It was to be built on the Potomac River and given the name Washington, D.C. Still, the quarreling continued. Finally, Jefferson had enough. In 1793, he submitted his formal resignation to Washington and set off for home. But three years later, in 1796, he was back in Philadelphia (the capital while Washington, D.C. was being built) running in the presidential election. He represented the Republican Party (today called the Democratic Party). His opponent was John Adams, who represented the Federalists. Adams won by 71 electoral votes to Jefferson's 68. By coming in second, Jefferson was elected vice-president. He brought with him to the inauguration a scientific paper on an ancient giant sloth that had recently been discovered in a Virginia cave. He also brought the bones! This was because he was also sworn into office as president of the American Philosophical Society at the same time.

During Jefferson's term of office as vice-president, he prepared for the next presidential election. He carefully organized his supporters and Republican leaders in each state. When it was time for the election of 1800, the Republicans were ready to carry the fight to every farm and village. And what a fight it was! It was the bloodiest campaign in American history. Jefferson's opponents insulted him in every way they could to turn voters against him. They lied about his conduct when he was governor of Virginia and called him a coward. Jefferson ignored the insults. But John Adams, who was running for reelection, was angered by the tactics. He said openly that Jefferson was the most qualified to be president. Because of Adams's loyalty and the strength of the political party founded by Jefferson, Jefferson won the election and became the third president of the United States.

During Jefferson's first term as president, he set about undoing policies that he felt were dictatorial, including the Alien and Sedition Acts which were passed by Congress in 1798. The Alien Act allowed the president to expel any alien he judged "dangerous to the peace and safety of the United States." He did the same with the Sedition Act, which made it a crime for anyone to say or publish anything against the government of the United States. In addition, he influenced the repeal of a whiskey tax and other unfair taxes that had been enacted by the Federalists. Jefferson also took measures to reduce the national debt by three million dollars a year. His greatest foreign policy success was the Louisiana Purchase, on April 30, 1803. On that date, the one-million-acre province of Louisiana was purchased from France for $12,000,000. Suddenly, the United States was twice as big! Because of all this, it is no wonder Jefferson was elected for a second term, in 1804, with a victory of 162 to 14 electoral votes.

Jefferson's second term included planning and organizing the Lewis and Clark expedition across the continent. Jefferson had gotten Congress to finance it. He chose his private secretary, Meriwether Lewis, to lead it. Lewis in turn, chose an experienced frontier soldier, William Clark, to accompany him. Then Jefferson arranged to have Lewis coached in astronomy, botany, mineralogy, cartography, zoology, and Native American history. In the spring of 1804, the two young Virginians, Lewis and Clark, set off on the expedition. They returned two and one half years later, having crossed the continent to the Pacific Ocean. While they were away, they sent Jefferson relics which he displayed in the East Room of the White House where various inventions were also displayed. Some of the inventions were Jefferson's, for he was often at work on some gadget or another. He invented for use at the White House a rotating clothes rack and a circular shelf that could turn into the next room with the flick of a switch. He was also the first president to install a running-water system in the White House by placing a water tank on the roof.

In 1808, Jefferson declined to run for a third term. But he made no secret of his choice for a successor—his longtime friend and secretary of state, James Madison. Madison scored an overwhelming victory. After attending the inauguration, Jefferson packed his belongings and rode out of Washington on March 11, 1809, never to return. At home, surrounded by his many grandchildren, Jefferson settled happily into his new life. He attended to his debts on his farms and continued to improve Monticello, by then a thirty-five room mansion. He continued to add to his marvelous collection of books that he had acquired since his first library was destroyed by the fire at Shadwell. Then, when the city of Washington was burned by the British during the War of 1812, Jefferson performed a noble act. He sold his treasure of books to Congress to replace the congressional library, which was destroyed in the fire. They became the foundation for today's Library of Congress collection. After that, from 1816-1819, Jefferson devoted himself to establishing the University of Virginia at Charlottesville. He had been concerned with education all his life and considered the founding of the University of Virginia his greatest achievement. He dedicated the University to the belief that truth makes people free.

Epilogue

Jefferson's final years were difficult ones. He was faced with many debts. He sold property and took out bank loans, but every year the situation got worse. Finally his grandson had to organize a lottery in the North to save Monticello from the auction block. Then on July 4, 1826—the fiftieth anniversary of the Declaration of Independence—Thomas Jefferson, at eighty-three, died at Monticello. His last words to his doctor and everyone else gathered at his bedside were, "Is it the Fourth?" (By an amazing coincidence, his loyal friend, John Adams, died that very day.) He was buried the next day in the family plot under a great oak tree. He had requested that the following words be inscribed on his tombstone:

Here was buried
Thomas Jefferson
April 13, 1743—July 4, 1826
Author of the Declaration of American Independence
of the Statute of Virginia for religious freedom
and Father of the University of Virginia.

Soon after Jefferson died, Monticello was sold. For a number of years it was abandoned. Then, in 1923, it was bought and artfully restored by a foundation. It is now a national shrine that is open to the public. Thousands of people visit Monticello every year and pay tribute to one of the truly great founders of America, an honorable and courageous man of many talents.